101 Amazing Things to Do in Rajasthan

© 2018 101 Coolest Things

All rights reserved. No part of this publication may be reproduced, distributed, or transmitted in any form or by any means, including photocopying, recording, or other electronic or mechanical methods, without the prior written permission of the publisher, except in the case of brief quotations embodied in critical reviews and certain other noncommercial uses permitted by copyright law.

Introduction

So you're going to Rajasthan, huh? You are very very lucky indeed! You are sure in for a treat because Rajasthan is truly one of the most magical places on this earth.

We will take you on a journey through all of the most popular places across Rajasthan, such as Jaipur, Jodhpur, Jaisalmer, Pushkar, Udaipur, Bundi, and even some very off the beaten track places.

In this guide, we'll be giving you the low down on:
- the very best things to shove in your pie hole, from street food staples like hot sweet jalebis through to gourmet rooftop restaurants
- the best shopping so that you can take a little piece of Rajasthan back home with you, whether that's in the form of an authentic block printed textiles or incredible local spices
- incredible festivals, whether you'd prefer to celebrate in Udaipur for the colourful Holi festivities, or you fancy taking in the atmosphere of the Pushkar Camel Fair

- the coolest historical and cultural sights that you simply cannot afford to miss from ancient fortresses through to amazing Royal Palaces
- outstanding experiences in nature from hiking in the Aravilla Hills, through to riding on a zipline in front of a palace
- and tonnes more coolness besides!

Let's not waste any more time – here are the 101 most amazing, spectacular, and cool things not to miss in Rajasthan!

1. Go Hot Air Ballooning Over Ranthambore National Park

India is a truly stunning country, but you can only appreciate how beautiful it is to a certain extent if you are viewing the country on a street level. To get a different perspective on its beauty, it can be a wonderful idea to take to the skies with a hot air balloon ride. There are numerous parts of the country where this is offered, but we like to ride the skies over Ranthambore National Park around Jaipur. From the balloon, you will see spectacular forts, rocky mountains, grasslands, the desert, as well as village life from a great height.

2. Visit the Largest Fort in India, Chittorgarh Fort

Dating way back to the 17th century, Chittorgarh Fort is one of the largest forts in all of India, and it's a must visit for all history buffs. This fort alone covers an area of more than 700 acres, and the fort has managed to survive three major battles over the course of its history. Inside, you will find an incredible array of temples and palaces that warrant at least a day of your time to see the place inside and out. In the evening, one of the towers become illuminated, and is nothing short of breath taking.

(Meera Nagar, Chittorgarh)

3. Take Some Kagzi Pottery Back Home With You

India is a country full of artisans, and as you walk around the shops and discover the handicrafts, you'll no doubt want to take a few pieces back with you. Whatever you do, do not miss out on the Kagzi pottery, which traditionally comes from a town called Alwar in Rajasthan. The style of this pottery is paper thin and biscuit coloured, with intricate engravings. Just be sure to travel to Alwar to get your hands on the real thing.

4. Stroll Through the City Palace of Jaipur

Jaipur has to be one of the most majestic and grand cities in all of India, and this is in no small part down to the City Palace. This incredible complex of courtyards, gardens, and buildings might actually take longer than a day to explore. Once inside, you will find a striking blend of Rajasthani and Mughal architecture, a collection of incredible shawls and pashminas, an art gallery, copies of sacred Hindu scriptures, a weapons collection, and many beautiful gardens for when you need some fresh air.

(Jaleb Chowk, Near Jantar Mantar, Tripolia Bazar, Jaipur)

5. Laugh Yourself Happy With a Laughter Yoga Class

Everybody knows what yoga is, but have you ever heard of laughter yoga? Well, this recent form of yoga is becoming popular in the big cities of India where people are searching for ways to escape the stresses of city living, and wish to discover the lighter side of life. The basic idea is that you join a group of people who spend half an hour to an hour just roaring with laughter. It might sound bizarre, but don't knock it 'til you've tried it.

6. Sip on Masala Tea Until You Burst

Something that will become very apparent on a trip to India is that the local people certainly do enjoy a cup of tea. The most common form of tea that is drank is simply black tea made with lots of milk and lots of sugar, but if you fancy ramping up your tea appreciation, we can heartily recommend a cup of masala tea. In the west, this might be called chai tea, but as chai translates as tea that literally makes no sense. Some of the spices you will taste in the tea include ginger, cardamom, cloves, and cinnamon. Perfect with breakfast!

7. Spend a Day Exploring the Amer Fort Outside of Jaipur

There is a huge amount to explore in and around Jaipur, but without a doubt, the number one attraction is the Amer Fort, a fort located high on a hill that overlooks Maota Lake. The fort is largely comprised of a stunning royal palace that has four courtyards, and it is famous for its artistic elements of Hindu style. You'll get to see a stairway with columns and incredible galleries, maharajas' apartments with beautiful frescoed arches and marble relief panels, and you may also relax outside in the gardens.

(Devisinghpura, Amer, Jaipur)

8. Visit a Camel Breeding Farm in Rajasthan

When you think of the desert and Rajasthan, your mind will probably wander to the majestic desert animals, camels, sooner or later. Well, while in the state, you can learn more about the animal on a camel breeding farm in

Bikaner. Once inside the farm, you can experience a camel ride, or something more unique, you can eat an ice cream made from the milk of camels. Would you dare?

(Jodhpur Bypass, Bikaner; www.nrccamel.res.in)

9. Celebrate Holi in Udaipur

In Udaipur, the vast majority of local people identify as Hindus, and this means that this city is a wonderful place to experience colourful Hindu festivals such as Holi. Many people around the world have some familiarity with the coloured paints of the Holi celebrations, but might not have experienced it first hand or understand the festival's significance. Visit Udaipur during March and you will get to see the festivities for yourself, which represent fertility, colour, love, and the triumph of good over evil.

10. Eat Hot Jalebis From the Street

Whenever you sip on a cup of tea in India, you understand that the local people certainly have a sweet tooth, and so it should come as no surprise that there are many sweet and sticky desserts to be found around the country. One of our favourite street desserts is definitely the jalebi.

Essentially, a wheat flour batter is piped into spiralling shapes in piping hot oil so that it resembles a pretzel, and it is then soaked in sugar syrup. These are best sampled hot from the fryer.

11. Traverse the Thar Desert by Jeep

The Thar Desert, also known as the Great Indian Desert, covers a staggering 320,000 square of land in Rajasthan and beyond. In fact, it takes up 90% of Rajasthan state, and this desert and its dunes are extremely hard to explore solo. The best way of exploring is definitely by Jeep, and there are many tour companies that can help you on your journey. It's only with a Jeep that you can reach the crest of the desert's highest dune and really experience the full majesty of this part of India.

12. Take a Morning Walk Around Bhatner Fort

If you would like to get a little bit off the beaten track while you are in Rajasthan, pay a visit to a town called Hanumangarh, which is more than 400 kilometres from the state capital, Jaipur. This is where you can find the Bhatner Fort, a very special place because it is thought to be around 1800 years old, making it one of the oldest forts not just in Rajasthan but the whole country. Take a stroll around in the morning time, and avoid the Rajasthani sun.

13. Watch a Puppet Show at the Thar Heritage Museum

When in Jaisalmer, you will probably be more interested in exploring the desert and the incredible forts than walking around museums, but if you do happen to be a culture vulture, we think that the Thar Heritage Museum will be right up your street. You'll find an assortment of local artefacts, such as musical instruments, turbans, and more. But the real highlight is the puppet show in the evening time that is sure to keep you entertained.

(Gandhi Chowk, Jaisalmer)

14. Fill Your Stomach With Bhel Puri From the Street

It goes without saying that India is one of the best places in the world for chowing down, and the street food is some of the best food that you can find. One of our favourite things to eat from the street is definitely Bhel Puri, and it's the perfect snack for when you're between meals and you want something tasty to tide you over. Bhel Puri is basically puffed rice with vegetables and a tangy tamarind sauce. You'll be back for seconds, we can guarantee it.

15. Take Part in the Kite Festival at Jodhpur

What could possibly be more beautiful than looking above you and seeing a sky full of meandering kites? Well, that's exactly what you can experience if you visit the annual Desert Kite Festival in Jodhpur, which takes place in the middle of January every year. The very best kite flyers from India, and indeed around the world, are invited to Jodhpur to take part in the celebrations. This festival is particularly popular with kids.

16. Cool Down With a Fresh Lassi

The heat in Rajasthan can be staggeringly warm, and with very little AC found (unless you want to pay a premium for it), you'll be looking for every possible opportunity to cool down. One of the most refreshing drinks to be found in India is the lassi. This drink is essentially a blend of yoghurt, water, and then some kind of flavourings. Locals often just drink it with a little salt, but you can go for mango or pistachio if you feel like something more decadent.

17. Have an Artsy Morning at the Anokhi Museum of Hand Painting

India is a country with a vibrant arts culture, and this is something that can be discovered at the Anokhi Museum of Hand Painting in Jaipur. This museum is very niche and chronicles the art of hand-block printing from ancient times right up to contemporary practices. Once inside, we are certain that you will be mesmerised by the intricate carvings that you can see happen in person. You can even have a go at carving and printing your very own block, and printing your own scarf or t-shirt.

(Anokhi Haveli, Near Badrinath Temple, Kheri Gate, Amber, Jaipur; www.anokhi.com/museum/home.html)

18. Witness the Incredible Pushkar Camel Fair

If there is one annual event in India that you should try to attend, we reckon it's the Pushkar Camel Fair, which is one of the largest camel fairs in the world. Now, if the idea

of trading camels doesn't sound all that appealing, this five day affair actually contains much more fun than just that. You will find live music with lots of singing and dancing, handicrafts stalls where you can find really special items, and even crazy competitions such as longest moustache competition. It takes place in Pushkar every November.
(www.pushkarcamelfair.com)

19. Explore the Stunning Mehrangarh Fort

One of the highlights of visiting the blue city of Jodhpur has to be a trip to the incomparable Mehrangarh Fort, a fortress that stands majestically on a rocky hill, and that can be seen from all over the city. This fort dates way back to the 15th century, and inside you can find seven ornately decorated palaces. There is also a museum inside with many stunning objects, including a collection of fine and applied arts from the Mughal period, beautiful armoury, a turban gallery, a paintings gallery, and more besides.
(P.B No 165, The Fort, Jodhpur, Rajasthan; www.mehrangarh.org)

20. Take a Camel Safari Through the Desert

Rajasthan is a state that has 90% desert, which can make it a little bit difficult to navigate unless you are travelling by train between the major cities. But if you want to experience the vast expanse of the Thar Desert itself, we can highly recommend taking a camel safari. There are numerous tour companies that provide these tours, and the most popular of these start in Jaisalmer. Some tours will simply take you out for half a day, whereas others cover multiple days, and you can camp overnight in the desert.

21. Visit the Under Appreciated Gagron Fort

If you're a fortress fanatic, there's no doubt that you have made it to the right part of India for you. And if you fancy seeing something a little off the beaten track, outside of the main cities, consider the underrated Gagron Fort, which you'll find 7 kilometres north of Jhalawar. The history of this place goes way back to the 8th century, and it's changed hands many times since then. There's a lot to explore so plan to spend the whole day there.

(http://tourism.rajasthan.gov.in/jhalawar)

22. Watch a Gypsy Snake Dance in Jodhpur

If you are in the beautiful blue city if Jodhpur in the evening time, and you are stuck for something to do, we can certainly recommend taking in authentic snake dance show. This part of Rajasthan is home to the Kalbeliya gypsy tribe, and it is typical for the women of this tribe to entertain with a gypsy folk dance involving snakes. In the past, this dance was entertainment for the Maharajah, and it can now be found in hotels in the evening.

23. Spend the Night in an 18th Century Palace

In India, there is an accommodation option to suit everybody, and if you really want to experience a touch of decadence, you'll be interested to know that there are quite a few palace hotels across the country. Taj Lake Palace has earned a reputation as the most romantic hotel in the whole world, and when you stay there it's easy to see why. This 18th century palace seems to be floating in the middle of Lake Pichola in Udaipur. It's a place to really get away from it all.

(Pichola, Udaipur, Rajasthan; https://taj.tajhotels.com/en-in/taj-lake-palace-udaipur)

24. Have an Artsy Day at Jawahar Kala Kendra

If you are an artsy, creative type of person, a place that you simply have to check out while in Jaipur is Jawahar Kala Kendra, a multi arts centre that was created by the local government to preserve and promote the arts of Rajasthan. Inside, you can find museums, an amphitheatre,
a library, galleries, an art studio, and even a hostel where you might want to stay. Keep your eyes peels on their programme of events if you want to catch something like a folk concert or an exhibition opening.

(2 Jawahar Lal Nehru Marg, Jhalana Doongri, Jaipur; www.jawaharkalakendra.rajasthan.gov.in)

25. Indulge a Sweet Tooth With Kulfi

India is certainly more famous for its savoury curries than for its sweet treats, but if you do have a sweet tooth, we can guarantee that this country isn't going to disappoint. When we need a sugar fix, we always go straight for a bowl of delicious kulfi. You can think of kulfi as the Indian version of ice cream, but it has some important differences. It is normally much denser and creamier than regular ice cream, and can be flavoured with deliciousness such as pistachio, mango, rose, cardamom, saffron, and more besides.

26. Celebrate Diwali, the Festival of Lights, in Jaipur

One of the most important celebrations of the year in India is Diwali, otherwise known as the Festival of Lights. Diwali is an ancient Hindu festival that is celebrated at the end of October each year, and it signifies the victory of light over darkness, good over evil, and knowledge over ignorance. Honestly, it's a wonderful festival to celebrate in many parts of the country, but it's particularly special in Jaipur where there are illuminated markets throughout the celebrations.

27. Climb the Iswari Minar Swarga Sal

When you are in Jaipur, something that you are bound to see, piercing the skyline above the city, is the Iswari Minar Swarga Sal. This strange looking minaret was created in the 1740s, and you can spiral all the way to the top for unbeatable views across the Pink City. This is one of the only viewpoints where you can actually take in a 360 degree panorama, so the climb to the top is definitely worth it.

(54, Tripolia Bazar, J.D.A. Market, Tripolia Bazar, Kanwar Nagar, Jaipur)

28. Shop for Jewellery at Johari Bazaar

Before you depart from the pink city of Jaipur, you'll no doubt want to take away some souvenirs that will always remind you of this jewel of Rajasthan. We think that one of the best places for a spot of morning shopping has to be Johari Bazaar, and the market is particularly well known for its jewellery. You can find anything and everything in the jewellery world, so whether you want gold, silver, diamonds, or precious stones such as amethysts and rubies, you are sure to find something you love.

(Johari Bazar Rd, Ramganj Bazar, Jaipur; www.johribazaar.com)

29. Indulge With a Decadent Meal at Suvarna Mahal

One of the highlights of visiting India is that even the most budget conscious travellers can afford to eat delicious meals there, but sometimes you just want to throw caution to the wind and eat in a really fancy restaurant, and when that moment arises we recommend reserving a table at Suvarna Mahal in Jaipur. The royal banquet hall is mesmerising, and the food is just as impressive. We recommend the tasting menu so you can try a little bit of everything.

(Taj Rambagh Palace, Bhawani Singh Road, Jaipur)

30. Visit the Fort of the Bikaner Royal Family

Located in the underrated city of Bikaner, the Junagarh Fort dates all the way back to the 16th century, a huge fort precinct that is studded with palaces, temples, and pavilions. A lot has been added to this fortress complex over the centuries, which means that when you visit you can see a broad mix of architectural styles in one place. Do pay the entrance for the fortress museum because it is filled with all manner of treasures, such as dresses, utensils, weapons, and musical instruments.

(Junagarh Fort Road, Bikaner; http://junagarh.org)

31. Sip on a Luxurious Falooda Drink

Falooda is part drink, part dessert that is extremely popular in warm places, and honestly, we can't think of any better way of cooling down than tucking into one of these bad boys. Falooda is a mix of rose syrup, vermicelli noodles, milk with gelatin, and basil seeds. It might sound like an odd combination but trust us when we say that it totally works and you'll be sipping on more than one of these during your time in India.

32. Traverse Kumbhalgarh Fort, the Great Wall of India

The Kumbhalgarh fort is no ordinary place, and if you are really interested in the local history, you could actually spend weeks and weeks exploring the place. It was constructed in the 15th century over the course of fifteen years, and has 36 kilometres of defensive walls, the second longest wall in the world next to the Great Wall of China. There's more than 360 temples inside the fortress, 300 of which are Jain, and the rest Hindu.
(http://tourism.rajasthan.gov.in/37/kumbhalgarh-fort)

33. Explore a Living Fort in Jaisalmer

The vast majority of the forts that you visit while in Rajasthan (and there will be a lot of them!) will be grand but historic buildings – a relic of the state's great past. But Jaisalmer Fort is something really quite different, because people actually live there today, so it feels like a living and breathing space. About 3000 live inside the walls of the fortress, which has cute winding lanes, shops, and houses throughout.

(Fort Road, Near Hanuman Circle, Amar Sagar Pol, Jaisalmer; http://tourism.rajasthan.gov.in/jaisalmer#jaisalmer-fort)

34. Climb to the Top of Nahargarh Fort

Jaipur is a really stunning, if rather hectic city. One way to get away from the crowds and to really appreciate the stunning beauty and scale of Jaipur is to pay a visit to Nahargarh Fort, which stands on a hilltop on the edge of the city. It was built way back in the 18th century, and once formed a strong defence for Jaipur. You are welcome to explore the stunning stucco details of the interiors, and then take in the sunset view of the Pink City.

(Krishna Nagar, Brahampuri, Jaipur)

35. Have a Rock Climbing Adventure at Mount Abu

Mount Abu is a popular hill station among the Aravalli Hills in Rajasthan. It's a wonderful place if you just want to relax, do some hiking, and enjoy some of the state's coolest temperatures. But if you are more adventurous than that, this is also the perfect place to enjoy a spot of rock climbing. There are awesome volcanic rock formations there, and many spots are ideal for beginners, so don't worry if you don't have climbing experience.

36. Explore Shekhawati, the Open Art Gallery of Rajasthan

Shekhawati in the north of Rajasthan, a region of the state, is a place that is not often visited by tourists, because it doesn't have the big forts, and the temperatures are extreme. But we think that it's well worth getting off the beaten track and checking this place out, particularly for its painted havelis, which date to the early 19th century, and make the whole place seem like an open-air art gallery. This region lies on an ancient caravan route, and the painted mansions point to the huge amount of wealth that Shekhawati used to enjoy.

37. Visit the Impressive Ranthambore Fort

Ranthambore National Park is a place where you can enjoy some greenery and nature, but history buffs needn't be left out, because the Ranthambore Fort also sits there. The date of the fort's construction is unknown, but it is thought to date all the way back to the mid-10th century. The inside of the fort takes up 4 square kilometres, with temples reservoirs, cenotaphs, stepwells, and barracks inside. The Ganesha Temple is a place to seek blessings of happiness and prosperity.

38. Eat a Tea Time Snack of Kalmi Vada

Travelling around Rajasthan can take up a lot of your energy, and so you might find yourself eating more than normal. When you want a snack between breakfast or lunch or lunch and dinner, something local and very very tasty is called Kalmi Vada. These are very simple spice lentil fritters that are served up with a fiery green chilli sauce for dipping. Although these are just a snack, we love them so much that we'd make a whole meal out of them.

39. Spend the Night in a Historic Fort

Rajasthan is a part of India that is full to the brim with the most incredible fortresses. But did you know that not all of these fortresses are relics of the past, and that you can actually pass the night in a special few? Fort Khejarla is one such place. This 400 year old structure combines epic history with modern luxury. This is one of the most unique ways to enjoy the desert landscape, in totally opulent style.

(Pipar Borunda Rd, Khejarla; http://jodhpurfortkhejarla.com)

40. Eat a Typical Rajasthani Curry, Laal Maas

The food in Rajasthan is incredible, and if you are a keen meat eater, one of the dishes you will want to eat again and again is called Laal Maas. This mutton curry is native to Rajasthan, and is positively bursting with savoury flavour. The mutton is served in a fiery red sauce that's made with Mathania chillies and yoghurt, and also contains a lot of garlic. It is traditionally mopped up with wheat flatbreads like chapatis or rotis.

41. Indulge a History Buff at the Ahar Museum

For all history enthusiasts, one of the museums that is a must-visit in Rajasthan is the Ahar Museum in Udaipur. This archaeological museum is filled with a plethora of incredibly fascinating objects, such as antiques, sculptures, coins, earthen pots, terracotta toys, and lots more besides. The most notable object within the museum is a 10th century metal figure of the Buddha.

(Ganapati Nagar, Udaipur;
www.udaipur.org.uk/excursions/ahar.html)

42. Take a Boat Ride on Fateh Sagar Lake

Rajasthan can be a hectic place to visit to say the least. There are lots of tourists, and the noise and pace of local life can also get pretty crazy. So what better way to unwind and find some peace than to visit a beautiful lake within the state? Fateh Sagar Lake is an artificial lake in Udaipur that offers welcome respite from the bustle of the city. The views around the lake are gorgeous, and you can even take boat trips on the water.

43. Take in a View of Jaipur from Jaigarh Fort

Forts are designed as buildings of defence and protection, but what happens when you need to protect the fort itself? You build yet another fort, of course! And that's exactly what Jaigarh Fort was built for – as protection of the Amer Fort next door. This is also one of the forts of Rajasthan that has kept its condition very well, and so you can really feel the place come to life as you walk around. The fort contains the world's largest cannon on wheels, and has incredible gardens and a museum.
(http://tourism.rajasthan.gov.in/jaipur#jaigarh-fort)

44. Eat a Bowl of Rajasthani Kadhi

Because the temperatures in Rajasthan can be exceedingly hot, yoghurt or curd are cooling ingredients that are very popular in Rajasthani cooking. One of our favourite yoghurt based dishes in the state is called Rajasthani Kadhi, which you can think of as a simple spiced yoghurt sauce. The sauce is spiced with things like turmeric, chillies, some chickpea flour, cumin, and fenugreek, and all the deliciousness is mopped up with rotis.

45. Take a Safari Through Sariska Tiger Reserve

Rajasthan is best known for its majestic fortresses, and its beautiful cities, but nature lovers still have plenty to enjoy on a trip to this historic state, and if you love greenery and the outdoors, be sure to include a trip to Sariska Tiger Reserve on your Rajasthan itinerary. The way to get around the park is with a jeep safari, because there's a lot of wild animals there that you wouldn't want get face to face with. Some of the animals in the park include leopards, Bengal tigers, hyenas, and jackals, among many others.

(Subhash Chowk Station road malakhera, Alwar; http://wildtrails.in/sariska)

46. Take in all the Glory of Hawa Mahal

Jaipur is a city that is brimming with majestic beauty, and perhaps the most iconic landmark in the whole city is the Hawa Mahal, a pink palace that was created in 1799 to allow female members of the Royal family to watch the goings on of the city. This is not just something to admire from the outside, but you can venture inside too (although the cramped alleyways can be a little claustrophobic). From the top, you'll experience a killer view.

(Hawa Mahal Rd, Badi Choupad, J.D.A. Market, Kanwar Nagar, Jaipur; www.hawa-mahal.com)

47. Catch a Show at the Rajasthan International Folk Festival

Held at the beautiful Mehrangarh Fort in Jodhpur, the Rajasthan International Folk Festival is an annual festival that takes place in October, and the programme is filled with all kinds of fascinating and entertaining performances. You will find dance and music performances of all kinds, but as you will have guessed from the name of the festival, you are likely to see a lot of folk performances – a great opportunity to get to know Rajasthani culture.

(www.jodhpurriff.org)

48. Meet Local Hipsters at Curious Life in Jaipur

When you think of Rajasthan, you probably don't think of lens free spectacles and trendy haircuts, but the hipster movement has even found its way to Jaipur! If you are desperate for an injection of some trendiness, and incredible coffee to boot, make sure that you make it to

Curious Life while you're in Jaipur. You can have your coffee made in all kinds of different ways, so whether you're into Aeropress, French Press, or V60 pour over, the choice is yours.
(P 25, Yudhisthir Marg, C Scheme, Jaipur; www.curiouslifecoffee.com)

49. Pick up Souvenirs at Rajasthali

Before you leave Rajasthan and head back home, you will surely want to pick up a few souvenirs from your trip, for yourself and for friends and family. There are lots of places for this, but most of the tourist shops sell overpriced items of poor quality. Take our advice and head to a shop called Rajasthali in Jaipur instead. This is a government run store, with everything from textiles to wood carvings, and jewellery to puppets.
(Mirza Ismail Road, Jayanti Market, Pink City, Jaipur; www.rajasthancrafts.gov.in)

50. Learn Something New in Jaipur's Albert Hall Museum

Rajasthan can be thought of as a living museum, with so many historic buildings and ruins that you can visit in the open air, but if you'd like to get some context to what you see across the state, a trip to the Albert Hall Museum in Jaipur can be very useful. Inside, you will find thousands of items pertaining to Rajasthani history and culture, such as clothing, jewellery, household items, and weapons. The highlight for us is the collection of ceramic art.
(Ajmeri Gate, Ramniwas Bag, Jaipur; http://alberthalljaipur.gov.in)

51. Eat Plenty of Gujia During Holi

As there are many Hindus throughout Rajasthan, it's a great idea to celebrate the Holi Festival in March there if you can. As well as lots of colour and music, you can expect particular foods that are eaten just for the festival. One that we are particularly enamoured by is called Gujia, and you can think of it as a kind of sweet dumpling. The case is made from a type of local wheat flour, and the filling is either thick condensed milk or a type of sweet coconut filling.

52. Be Wowed by Carved Stone Monuments at Royal Gaitor

Jaipur is a pretty hectic city to say the least, but just on the edge of the city you can find the Royal Cenotaphs, a place that is not quite so visited by tourists as the main attractions, and where you won't be elbowing people out of the way. And they are really very spectacular. This vast funerary complex holds the tombs of the ruling family of Jaipur, going all the way back to the city's founder, who was laid to rest there in the 18th century.

(Krishna Nagar, Brahampuri, Jaipur)

53. Buy Block Printed Clothes From Inde Rooh

Rajasthan is a place that people from all over the world visit to see its incredible fortresses and to check out the desert landscapes, but there's also an incredible arts and crafts scene here, particularly when it comes to textiles. Block printing by hand is something that is very popular across the state, and if you'd like to take some beautiful textiles back home with you, we recommend taking a trip to a shop called Inde Rooh in Jaipur. There is both menswear and womenswear, and absolutely everything inside the shop is hand stitched and hand printed.

(51 Hathroi Fort Hari Kishan Somani Marg, Ajmer Road, Jaipur; www.inderooh.com)

54. Get Decadent With Delicious Mawa Kachori

The curries of India are more famous than the desserts, but if you have a sweet tooth, fear not, because Mawa Kachori is something that comes from Rajasthan, and is totally sweet and decadent. This is a crispy pastry that has the flavour of cardamom, almonds, and pistachio, is filled with cream, and is then covered in a sugar syrup.

55. Watch a Movie at the Raj Mandir Cinema

There's certainly no shortage of things to see and do across Rajasthan, but travel can be exhausting, and there could just be some moments when you need to kick back, relax, and watch a great movie. When that moment strikes, you should head for the Raj Mandir Cinema in Jaipur. The building itself looks like a giant pink cream cake, and is the best known cinema in all of Rajasthan. Catch a Hindi movie, and get to know this very unique part of the local culture.

(C-16, Bhagwan Das Rd, C-Scheme, Panch Batti, Jaipur; http://therajmandir.com)

56. Zip Line at the Neemrana Fort Palace

Ziplining is a super fun activity that adventure seekers love, and normally you would find zip lines in places like jungles, mountains, and adventure parks, but we had never seen one at a fortress before visiting the Neemrana Fort Palace, a gorgeous fortress that dates all the way back to the 15th century. As you zip down, you'll have amazing views of the palace, Neemrana village, and the surrounding hills.

(www.flyingfox.asia)

57. Discover a World of Vintage Cars in Udaipur

You probably didn't travel all the way to Rajasthan to indulge an obsession with cars, but if you do happened to be an automobile fanatic you are in luck as the Vintage & Classic Cars Museum in Udaipur will be right up your street. Inside, you are treated to a collection of 22 incredible vintage vehicles, including a 1934 Rolls Royce that was used in the Bond film, Octopussy, and a 1961

Cadillac convertible that Queen Elizabeth II once took a ride in.
(Gulab Bagh Road, Udaipur; www.eternalmewar.in/museums/vintage-classic-car-collection/index.aspx)

58. Enjoy the Festivities of Gangaur Festival

There is no doubt that the local people of Rajasthan love to celebrate a festival, and if you can plan your trip to coincide with the huge festival of Gangaur, your trip is guaranteed to be unforgettable. This is a festival that is unique to Rajasthan, and it celebrates spring, marriage and fidelity, and takes place in March or April each year. Women dress up in colourful clothes and pray for a good husband, there is a huge procession in big cities like Jaipur and Jodhpur, and you can also hear women singing Rajasthani folk songs.

59. Enjoy a Rooftop Dinner at Indique Restaurant

While in Rajasthan, there is no doubt that you can fill your stomach with all kinds of incredible deliciousness, but because eating out is really very reasonably priced, you don't have to eat in super expensive places to have a meal with a view. One of our favourite terrace restau in Jodhpur in Indique. This restaurant is located on the roof of the Pal Haveli Hotel, and with its candlelight and incredible views, is the perfect spot for a romantic evening with great food.

(pal haveli, Opp. Clock Tower Near, Gulab Sagar, Jodhpur; www.palhaveli.com/restaurant.php)

60. Shop at Jodhpur's Sardar Market

For us, one of the most fun ways to get to know a new place is to stroll the aisles of its local market. Rajasthan is a part of India with a very strong market culture, and one of the best and busiest markets you will find there is the Sardar market. This is a really fantastic place to purchase souvenirs before heading here, because you'll find things like embroideries, printed textiles, wood carvings, and ceramics, and without the hefty price tags of the tourist souvenir shops. Don't be afraid to haggle for the best price!

(Clock Tower, Girdi Kot Front Gate, Rawaton Ka Bass, Jodhpur)

61. Stay Overnight at Umaid Bhawan Palace

The Umaid Bhawan Palace is a very special place in Jodhpur as it was the last Royal Palace built in India before the Independence of India, with construction starting in 1929. The Taj Hotels Group owns a part of the palace now, so you can actually stay there, and the experience is just about as luxurious as it comes. There is an incredible spa where you can treat yourself to incredible Ayurvedic treatments, lavish dining, and even an outdoor space to enjoy a barbecue.

(Circuit House Rd, Cantt Area, Jodhpur; https://taj.tajhotels.com/en-in/umaid-bhawan-palace-jodhpur)

62. Take a Boat Trip to Jagmandir Island

Since Rajasthan is a land locked state, you probably wouldn't expect to have the opportunity to visit an island while you are there. But think again, because Jagmandir Island is located in the middle of Lake Pichola. If you are feeling fancy, you can stay at a Palace on the island that was built all the way back in 1620. With only seven hotel rooms, be sure to book your place in advance!

(Pichola, Udaipur, Rajasthan 313001)

63. Watch Rajasthani Folk Dance at Dharohar

While in Udaipur, be sure to pass at least one evening at a place called Dharohar, which puts on some of the best Rajasthani folk shows in the whole of the state. These shows are performed nightly, so there is absolutely no excuse not to check the place out. The dances are colourful and lively, and if you are taken by the performances, you can also sign up for dance classes there.
(23/186, "Bhagwat", Parshwanath Colony, Near Savina Vatika, Udaipur; www.dharoharfolkdance.com)

64. Learn About the Desert at Arna Jharna

One of the most unique things about Rajasthan is the incredible desert landscape that you will be face to face with everywhere that you go. A place where you can learn more about the desert is Arna Jharna in Jodhpur, which is also known as The Desert Museum. But don't think of this as another stuffy museum. This is an interactive outdoor space that depicts the lifestyle of people who live in the desert villages of Rajasthan.
(Near Arneshwar Mahadev Mandir, Arna Jharna, Jodhpur; www.arnajharna.org)

65. Get to Grips With Folk Art at Bharatiya Lok Kala Mandal

Bharatiya Lok Kala Mandal is the place to go in Udaipur for people who seriously love the arts. This is a cultural institution that is dedicated to studying the folk arts, festivals, and culture of Rajasthan. The museum is particularly strong on artefacts pertaining to Rajasthani folk art, including dresses, turbans, musical instruments, paintings, and puppets. Plus, there's daily puppet shows at 6pm, which are hugely popular with kids.

(Saheli Marg, Madhuban, Udaipur)

66. Visit an Abandoned Ghost Town

Just 20 kilometres outside of Jaisalmer, you will find a small, deserted town that goes by the name Kuldhara. This is a rather eerie place in Rajasthan, because it was abandoned by its inhabitants 200 years ago. The town was abandoned because it was put under a curse that expressed it would never be inhabited again – and indeed that curse has come true, as the remains of the buildings haven't been touched since those two centuries back. It is believed that the ghosts of the town still inhabit the ruins.

67. Learn Something New at the Government Museum Jhalawar

Jhalawar is a city in the south of Rajasthan state that you might not even have heard of before, but if you're a history buff, it's well worth paying a visit to this city, to visit its fort, as well as the Government Museum within the fort. This museum is one of the oldest museums in all of Rajasthan, and it opened way back in 1915. Inside you'll find architectural remains and sculptures retrieved from the fort, some great paintings, inscriptions, coins, and sculptures of Hindu deities.

(Garh Palace, Bhoj Mohalla, Jhalawar; http://tourism.rajasthan.gov.in/jhalawar)

68. Buy Artisanal Textiles From Sadhna

The textiles n Rajasthan are full of colour, often hand printed, and simply glorious. You will no doubt want to take some of the stunning local textiles back home with you, and Sadhna in Udaipur is a fantastic place to pick these up. The really incredible thing about this shop is that its actually an NGO, and everything on sale is produced by rural and tribal people who otherwise find it hard to sell their wares, and they are paid a very fair price for their work.

(Seva Mandir, Old Fatehpura, Udaipur; www.sadhna.org)

69. Spend a Morning at the Jaisalmer War Museum

The Jaisalmer War Museum is a very new museum in the state of Rajasthan, only recently opened in 2015 by the Indian Army, primarily to commemorate the soldiers of the Indo-Pak War, but there is a focus on many battles throughout history. Inside you will see impressive artefacts such as tanks, guns, and military vehicles, as well as information about local soldiers in wars throughout world history.

70. Visit the Haunted Bhangarh Fort

You are likely to visit a lot of fortresses while you are in Rajasthan, but the Bhangarh Fort has a story unlike any other, which has earned it the title of most haunted place in India. The king who created the fort declared that the

shadow must never fall upon the home of the ascetic, but when fortifications were added, it became engulfed by shadows. Since then, the place has been cursed – or so the story goes. Only visit after sunset if you are feeling particularly brave.
(Gola ka baas, Rajgarh Tehsil, Alwar, Bhangarh)

71. Feel Rejuvenated After an Ayurvedic Massage

If you are not familiar with Ayurveda, it is essentially a system of ancient medicine that has its roots in India. If you subscribe to the Ayurvedic way of healing, everything from diet to medicine to massage can transform your body and mind. And if you just fancy dipping your toe into this world, getting an Ayurvedic massage is a great idea. Many types of beautiful oils are used, and we guarantee that you will feel rejuvenated afterwards. Ayurveda centres can be found all over the state.

72. Watch the Processions of the Mewar Festival

Spring time is a wonderful time of year to be in the city of Udaipur, and this is not least because this is when the city celebrates its Mewar Festival to inaugurate the season.

This festival is celebrated in either March or April, and the whole city and its surrounding areas come to life with colour and festivities. This festival is especially significant for women who dress in their finest clothes during the days of the festival.

73. Visit an Ancient Mausoleum: Ahar

History buffs shouldn't miss the opportunity to visit Ahar, which lies around 3 kilometres outside of Udaipur, and is a spectacular cremation ground for the Udaipur Royals, comprising 372 cenotaphs of maharanas and Queens of Mewar. Many of he cenotaphs are made out of marble and are complete with many intricate carvings. This is the place where local people come to pay homage to their great rulers of the past.

74. Visit an Arts & Crafts Village, Shilpgram

Just 3 kilometres outside of the city of Udaipur, you can find an arts and crafts complex that goes by the name of Shilpgram. You can think of this as a museum village, filled with 26 traditional village houses that depict the local arts, crafts, lifestyle, and culture of various rural people.

This is a fantastic place to see hands on demonstrations and dance performances in a unique setting.
(www.shilpgram.in)

75. Escape City Life at Saheliyon-ki-Bari

Although Udaipur can be a hectic place, there are also some lovely green spaces that you can escape to when city life gets all too much. For us, the best of these parks is called Saheliyon-ki-Bari. This garden is not only beautiful but also historic as it was built by the ruler of Udaipur in the early 18th century. Stroll these gardens and you will be greeted with delightful fountains, lotus pools, and marble sculptures.

(Lake City, Near Science Museum, Udaipur)

76. Purchase Churma Ladoo from Sweet Shops

The people of Rajasthan have something of a sweet tooth, and the local sweet shops are wondrous places to visit with all kinds of desserts and sweet treats. One of our favourite sweet nibbles that is most common in Rajasthan and Gujurat is called Churma Ladoo. Churma is a sweet whole flour mixture, and this flour is then rolled into jaggery and ghee to create a sweet and succulent bite.

77. Visit a Jain Temple in Bikaner

Rajasthan is a place that is filled with stunning Jain temples, and we think that one of the most beautiful is Bhandasar Temple in Bikaner. This temple really stands out from the crowd because of its bright yellow colour and incredibly vibrant paintings. The temple was built in the 15th century, making it one of the oldest temples in Bikaner, and is still a popular pilgrimage destination today. Climb to the top for a killer view of Bikaner.

78. Shop for Clothes at Tripolia Bazaar

If you're a shopaholic through and through, there is one place that you simply have to visit while you are in Jaipur, and that is the Tripolia Bazaar. The thing we love about this particular market ad a shopping destination is that nothing is imported from around India, so absolutely everything on sale is Rajasthani in origin. You can pick up textiles, jewellery, ceramics, handicrafts, and loads more besides.

79. Go Birdwatching at Keoladeo National Park

The Keoladeo National Park is a place of very welcome respite from the busy cities of Rajasthan. This park used to be a duck hunting reserve for the maharajas of the state, and welcomes aquatic birds from places like China, Afghanistan, Turkmenistan, and Siberia in the winter months. Over 360 bird species have ben located in the park, including many rare varieties of birds, making it a must-visit destination for keen birdwatchers.

(Agra-Jaipur Highway, Bharatpur; http://tourism.rajasthan.gov.in/bharatpur/10014/keoladeo-ghana-national-park)

80. Shop for Spices at Jodhpur's MV Spices

It goes without saying that one of the best aspects of visiting Rajasthan is having the opportunity to tuck into all of its richly flavoured cuisine. And if you want to recreate some of the incredible local dishes when you are back home, you will certainly need a cupboard that is full of the incredible spices, like mustard seeds, coriander seeds, cumin, ginger, turmeric, curry leaves, dried chillies, and cardamom. And you can stock up on all of that at Jodhpur's MV Spices. The staff really know their stuff and will help you buy what you need.

(Shop No. 209B, Inside Sardar Market, Clock Tower, Jodhpur; www.mvspices.com)

81. Stroll the Chambal Garden

Located on the banks of the river Chambal in Kota, the Chambal Garden is a place to re-centre yourself and enjoy some much needed peace and quiet in bustling Rajasthan. There is a huge amount of flora and fauna that is native to Rajasthan in the gardens, so nature lovers and gardening enthusiasts will have a great time among the wildlife. Something else you won't fail to notice are the crocodiles that lounge around in the ponds of the garden.

82. Take the Kids to Birla City Water Park

Travelling with kids in Rajasthan can be quite a challenge. For starters, the heat can make them irritable, and secondly the state is full of historic and cultural attractions that are just not all that appealing to little ones. But one thing they will love is a day at the Birla City Water Park.

This is the best of the water parks in Rajasthan, and being surrounded by so much water is always a pleasure in the fierce Rajasthani sun. There are slides, pools, and waterfalls for the whole family to enjoy.
(Near Circle Makhupura 30502, Makhupura Industrial Area, Ajmer; http://birla-city-water-park.business.site)

83. Visit a Stunning Memorial Called Jaswant Thada
Jaswant Thada is something that you really shouldn't miss in Jhodpur. This architectural marvel is a gorgeous white marble cenotaph, built in 1899 to commemorate Maharaja Jaswant Singh II. The craftsmanship on display is second to none in the city, and the main memorial looks more like a temple than a cenotaph, with intricate carvings, wonderful sculptures, and spectacular domes. It's a peaceful spot in the city, with views across Jodhpur.

84. Visit the Abhaneri Stepwell
Chand Baori, otherwise known as the Abhaneri Stepwell, is one of the most spectacular stepwells to be found in all of Rajasthan. If you are unfamiliar with the concept of a stepwell, it is a well reached by descending a set of steps.

That might not sound like anything special, but trust us when we say that it's actually very intricately designed and surprisingly beautiful. This particular stepwell was constructed way back in the year 800, and contains 3500 narrow steps.

85. Visit an Historic Astrological Observatory, Jantar Mantar

Jantar Mantar in Jaipur is a place that will appeal to both history enthusiasts and science geeks alike, because this is an historic astrological observation site, built in the 18th century, with all of its original apparatus. There are 20 instruments in total, each of which serves a different purpose, and are very well maintained. This site is a true testament to the scientific prowess of the people of the Mughal period in this part of the world.
(Gangori Bazaar, J.D.A. Market, Kanwar Nagar, Jaipur)

86. Have a Luxurious Stay at Rambagh Palace

Rambagh Palace was built in the 19th century for the Maharaja of Jaipur, but these days it's a 5 star hotel, which means that you have the unique opportunity of staying in a

Royal Palace when you visit Rajasthan. Occupying a 47 acre plot just south of the city, this is the hotel you need if you have a taste for all things luxurious, and you want plenty of space. With incredible interiors and service that is truly second to none, it might just be worth splashing out for a couple of nights.
(Bhawani Singh Road, Jaipur; https://taj.tajhotels.com/en-in/taj-rambagh-palace-jaipur)

87. Take in a World of Crystal in Udaipur

The Crystal Gallery in Udaipur is a very special place because it contains the largest private collection of crystals, anywhere in the world. There is an incredible array of crystal objects, and you'll be able to find all kinds of things such as crystal bowls, ornaments, goblets, candle stands, decanters, crockery – and you can even get up close to a bed made from crystal. Pay a little extra for the audio guide if you really want to get to grips with everything in the museum.
(Jagdish Chowk, 3, City Palace Road, Rao Ji Ka Hata, Udaipur)

88. Have a Dune Bashing Adventure in Jaisalmer

Have a taste for wild adventure? You're in luck because Jaisalmer is the place where you can try your hand at dune bashing for the first time. If you're unfamiliar with the idea of dune bashing it's essentially a rollercoaster ride through the desert, and your vehicle of choice is a 4x4 vehicle. You'll have a well-practiced driver who will take reign of the steering wheel, and give you the ride of your life.

89. Take in the Glory of Patwon-ki-Haveli

If you aren't familiar with the word Haveli, it can be translated to mean mansion, and if you have a taste for the decadent and beautiful things in life, be sure to visit the Patwon-ki-Haveli in Jaisalmer. This is actually a complex of five separate havelis that are connected to each other, each of which has an incredibly intricate exterior, covered with balconies. You are welcome to enter and walk around, and many of the rooms have been furnished so they look as they would have at the turn of the 20th century.

(Patwon ki Haveliyan, Jaisalmer)

90. Enjoy the Elephant Festival of Jaipur

The Elephant Festival is something unique to the city of Jaipur, and it is always celebrated on the day of Holi, which typically lands in the month of March. The festival begins with an incredible procession of elephants, camels, horses, and local folk dancers. All of the elephants are incredibly decorated with prizes for the most beautiful designs. You can also catch elephant polo, elephant races, and elephant tug of war competitions.

91. Visit the Beautiful Ranakpur Temple

Located in the western part of Rajasthan, Ranakpur is a town that many foreign travellers don't make it to, but it's totally worth making the effort to see this place if you are interested in temples because the Ranakpur Jain Temple is something very special indeed. A local businessperson started the construction of this temple in the 15th century after experiencing a Divine vision. It is created out of white marble, and contains many stunning pillars, carvings, and statues.

92. Understand Tribal India at Bishnoi Village

When you just visit the main cities of Rajasthan, you don't have a true picture of Rajasthani life, and that's why it's a great idea to get off the beaten track and visit some smaller places. Bishnoi, outside of Jodhpur, is a place that preserves tribal traditions, but that is also accessible to westerners because you can go on a Bishnoi Village Safari and take in local life with a helpful local guide. You'll get to see farmers, potters, weavers, and the local way of life in rural Rajasthan.

(www.bishnoivillagesafari.org/bishnoi_village_safari/index.html)

93. Tuck Into Vegetable Biryani in Jodhpur

One of the excellent things about Indian cuisine is that it caters to vegetarians exceptionally well. Truthfully, the people in Rajasthan do eat quite a lot of meat, but there's always something on restaurant menus for veggies, and you can't leave Jodhpur without trying their famous vegetable biryani, which is also known as Jodhpuri Kabuli. Basmati rice is layered with veggies such as potato, cauliflower, and onions, as well as many spices, and sometimes you can even find raisins and cashew nuts inside.

94. Stroll Around the Seven Wonders Park in Kota
The Seven Wonders of the World represent the grandest feats of architecture and design right around the globe, but getting to see all of these wonders up close is an expensive exercise. Fear not, because in Kota there is a place called the Seven Wonders Park where you can see each of the wonders in miniature. This isn't quite as cheesy as it sounds, because the stone craftsmanship of these miniatures is actually incredible, and worth a visit if you do happen to be in Kota.

95. Be Stunned by a 14th Century Fort in Ajmer
The city of Ajmer might be a place in Rajasthan that you haven't yet heard of, but if you want to take a comprehensive journey around the state, it's a place that shouldn't be missed out. The most impressive site in this city is the Taragarh Fort, otherwise known as the Star Fort. It was constructed all the way back in 1354, and thus has a lot of history behind and, in fact, this is widely believed to be the first ever hill fort in all of India.

96. Indulge a Sweet Tooth With Dil Kushar

If you've ever had a sip of Indian tea before, you will know that the local population is rather fond of sugar, and so you'll have no problem finding sweet treats during your time in Rajasthan. Enter any sweet shop in Rajasthan, and you will find delightful little morsels that go by the name of Dil Kushar. These are made from gram flour and ghee, and are flavoured with cardamom and almonds. They are often eaten for special occasions like weddings and festivals.

97. Trek Through the Aravalli Hills

When you think of Rajasthan, you certainly wouldn't think of green mountains, but Rajasthan is a large place and the landscapes totally change as you travel around. If you love hiking and greenery, you should certainly acquaint yourself with the Aravalli Hills. These hills are the hidden part of Rajasthan, and totally unspoiled by the 21st century. Remember to pack your hiking boots, and you'll have a wonderful time in the Aravalli Hills.

98. Indulge a Bibliophile at the Jaipur Literature Festival

If you are the kind of person who always has their head in the pages of a book, you might be interested in coinciding your Rajasthan trip with the Jaipur Literature Festival, which is hosted each year in January. This is actually the world's largest free literary festival, and there is plenty for bookworms to enjoy. Authors who have attended the event for panels, signings, and readings include Ian McEwan, Donna Tartt, and Vikram Seth, as well as many others.

(https://jaipurliteraturefestival.org)

99. Walk Through Rao Jodha Desert Rock Park

Nature lovers might think of going to the very green state of Kerala or the mountains of Himachel Pradesh before heading to Rajasthan, but there is plenty here for outdoor enthusiasts too, and the Roa Jodha Desert Park in Jodhpur should definitely be one that nature lovers visit. This 72 hectare park is very well put together, with flora and fauna that showcases the diversity of the region. Visit in the morning for the best temperatures, and visit with a local guide if you really want the inside track on everything that you see.

(www.raojodhapark.com)

100. Explore the Ruins of Jalore Fort

Jalore is a town of Rajasthan that you might not have heard about, but it actually contains one of the most impressive forts in the whole country. Nobody can be quite sure when the fort was built, but it's thought to date back to the 8th to 10th centuries. This fort is located up a steep hill, which takes about an hour to climb (do start early because the Rajasthani heat is fierce).

101. Celebrate at the Kolayat Fair

The Kolayat Fair is an annual festival that is hosted in Bikaner in November each year. What we love about this festival is the decorations that you will find across the 52 ghats in the city, which are lit up beautifully. You will see thousands of devotees of the Sankhya philosophy who descend upon the holy waters of Lake Kapil where they submerge themselves to wash away their sins.

Before You Go

Hey you! Thanks so much for reading **101 Amazing Things to Do in Rajasthan.** We really hope that this helps to make your time in Japan the most fun and memorable trip that it can be.

Have a great trip!
Team 101 Amazing Things

Made in the USA
Columbia, SC
31 August 2019